The Three Lives of Lucie Cabrol is a wild, tiny, peasant family in France in 1900. Abandoned by her lover, Jean, and banished by her family, she becomes an outcast. In this, her second life, she survives by smuggling goods across the border and by scavenging in the mountains. But it is not until her third life, her afterlife, that she discovers the survival of something more than bare human existence – the survival of hope and love.

The Three Lives of Lucie Cabrol, adapted from John Berger's short story, was first performed at the Manchester Dance-house in January 1994. It subsequently toured throughout Britain before a sell-out run at the Riverside Studios, London. In 1995 it was revived for a West End season at the Shaftesbury Theatre, London, and a further British and international tour.

'In Simon McBurney's exhilarating production the story becomes an unsentimental evocation of peasant life, a hymn to the tenacity of love and a Brechtian fable about the world's unfairness . . . Complicite's brilliant technique is used to express Berger's ideas . . . Complicite have matured into greatness.' Michael Billington, *Guardian*

'You follow this Complicite version [of John Berger's story] as intensely as you read a Grimms' fairytale.' Alastair Macaulay, *Financial Times*

'Complicite have given us a work that glows in the mind.' *The Times*

Simon McBurney is an actor, writer and Artistic Director of Theatre de Complicite. He studied at Cambridge and trained at the Jacques Lecoq School, Paris. His theatre work includes: opening night of the Comedy Store (London); *Notes of a Dirty Old Man* (Edinburgh Fringe First Award); *Strapontin* (Compagnie Jerome Deschamps – Paris, London and Avignon); *Eurydice* (Chichester). For Complicite: *Put It On Your Head, A Minute Too Late, More Bigger Snacks Now, Food Stuff, Please Please Please, Alice In Wonderland, Anything For A Quiet Life*; *The Visit* (Almeida/Riverside/Royal National Theatre); *My Army Part One and Two, The Winter's Tale*; *The Street of Crocodiles* (Olivier Award nomination for Best Director; Royal National Theatre and West End); *The Three Lives of Lucie Cabrol*; and *Out of a House Walked a Man* . . . (co-production with the Royal National Theatre). He has also directed and taught for many other companies, leading chorus work and 'Theatre Beyond Words' projects at the Royal National Theatre Studio. TV includes: *Burning Ambition* (writer/actor); *Anything For A Quiet Life* (adapter and co-director); *Stolen, Gregory, Diary of a Nutcase, The Crying Game* (Comic Strip); *The Vicar of Dibley*. Film includes: *Tom and Viv, Being Human, Mesmer, Business Affair, Kafka, The Vacuum*.

Mark Wheatley has been Literary Advisor to Theatre de Complicite since 1992. He has worked on *Help! I'm Alive* and *The Visit*, and co-adapted *The Street of Crocodiles* (Olivier Award nomination for Best Play), *The Three Lives of Lucie Cabrol* and *Out of a House Walked a Man* . . . (co-production with Royal National Theatre).

John Berger, born in London in 1926, is a novelist, playwright, documentary writer and art critic. His novels include *Pig Earth, Once in Europe* and *Lilac and Flag*. He won the Booker Prize for his novel *G.* in 1972. His books with the photographer Jean Mohr include *A Fortunate Man, A Seventh Man* and *Another Way of Telling*. He has written several books on art, including *Ways of Seeing* and *Success and Failure of Picasso*. He lives in a village in the French Alps.

The Three Lives of Lucie Cabrol

based on a story by
JOHN BERGER

adapted by
SIMON MCBURNEY *and* MARK WHEATLEY

and devised by
THEATRE DE COMPLICITE

METHUEN DRAMA

Methuen Modern Plays

2 4 6 8 10 9 7 5 3

First published in Great Britain 1995
by Methuen Drama
Random House, 20 Vauxhall Bridge Road,
London SW1V 2SA
and Australia, New Zealand and South Africa

Copyright © 1995 by Theatre de Complicite
The authors have asserted their moral rights

Random House UK Limited Reg. No. 954009

ISBN 0–413–69690–1

A CIP catalogue record for this book
is available at the British Library

Typeset by Wilmaset Ltd, Birkenhead, Wirral
Printed in Great Britain by
Cox & Wyman Ltd, Reading, Berkshire

Thanks are due to Michael Ratcliffe for permission to reprint the article on p. vi.

Front cover design by Russell Warren-Fisher; cover photogarph and production photographs inside the book by Hannes Flaschberger

Caution

John Berger on Theatre de Complicite

Lucie Cabrol was a smuggler. Theatre de Complicite are also smugglers in that they ignore frontiers and cross them without official papers. First they leave the stage to fetch the public – not once but a hundred times during a performance. Then they lead the public across their actions and their words – with an absolute minimum of luggage – to a foreign, unknown heartland. In *The Street of Crocodiles* this heartland was the imagination of a Polish Jew in Warsaw fifty years ago. In *The Three Lives of Lucie Cabrol* the heartland is the tenacity and love of a peasant woman, as old as our century, somewhere in the mountains of central Europe.

Thus this theatre smuggles the public in to places which are normally considered closed. And they smuggle out of those distant places the daily routines and the triumph and the pain of being alive, all of it stuff which, carried on their shoulders, in their voices and under their arms, is immediately recognisable and intimately familiar. Contraband nevertheless. Contraband because it's about what is habitually marginalised, dismissed, belittled, made voiceless. Maybe the essential contraband today is hope. Hope which is inseparable from life, like the violent theatre these gentle artists make.

Left to right: Henri, Mélanie, Émile and Lucie Cabrol in the original 1994 production

Collusion Between Celebrants
by Michael Ratcliffe

Theatre de Complicite is one of three intimate touring groups which quietly revolutionised British theatre and rendered it less insular during the course of the 1980s (the others are Shared Experience and Cheek by Jowl). Complicite's influence has been memorable in impact, spreading from their own brilliant but almost literally indescribable shows into productions at the Old Vic, English National Opera, the West End and the Royal National Theatre.

They are zealots and preach what they practise. They have worked with actors, directors, designers, peasants and children, and could no doubt make theatre with critics, audiences, programme-sellers and car-park attendants if required. In Oxford they drew a performance of *Romeo and Juliet* from thirty schoolchildren whose knowledge of the play had been simply that it had a party, a balcony, ballroom dancing and 'I love you' in it, and that everybody died at the end.

In Chile police scratched their heads in the middle of the road while the disruptive actors melted into the laughing crowd; motorists in Sao Paolo, driving too fast and wildly distracted by sidewalk performances, smashed up each other's cars. The actors swiftly transformed themselves into witnesses offering strident and spurious evidence as to what had occurred. Complicite – complicity – is a form of collusion between celebrants.

Like the performers of the Venetian *commedia dell'arte* whose work they honoured in *Help! I'm Alive* (1990), they are anarchists of the city: they speak for the urban dumbos, deadbeats and dispossessed in a world where ugliness is endemic and dignity a luxury confined to the rich. Again like the *commedia*, they animate a theatre of survival, the survival of the poor.

Founded in 1983 by Annabel Arden, Simon McBurney, Marcello Magni and the Canadian actress Fiona Gordon,

joined by the producer Catherine Reiser in 1986,
Complicite is a core-collective which visiting members
join, leave and re-join: the English rodent-intensity of
McBurney and the generous Latin explosiveness of Magni
are tempered, for example, by the startling and ethereal
Linda Kerr Scott; by ex-squaddie Tim Barlow (the one
who looks like Gladstone); or by Kathryn Hunter and Lilo
Baur, who in *Help!* played, respectively, a pot-bellied
businessman and the object of his desires, a tarty Italian
wife with filed teeth, stretching a Lycra dress where no
Lycra dress had ever gone before, and swinging
winsomely off a ceiling and two walls. Every actor who
plays with the company is individually eccentric, some
have star-quality, yet none disturbs the sanity of the
ensemble.

Many have studied in Paris with Jacques Lecoq, from
whom they learned that 'stage presence' – the truthfulness
of the actor in and with his own body – is no mystery
given or witheld at birth, but a skill to be taught and
learned. Intellectual and physical understanding are
separate disciplines: British performers are instinctively
good at the first, but find the second harder. The actor's
imagination creates theatre as much as those of the writer
or director – a faith more European than British to which
Complicite, like Peter Brook and Mike Alfreds (the
founder of Shared Experience), unquestioningly adheres.
Without the commitment of each actor to his colleagues,
the company, family and team would cease to be.

If these ideas have taken hold in the younger generation
of British actors, it is partly due to eleven years of classes,
workshops, and exemplary performances by Theatre de
Complicite.

The collective devises its own shows around a universal
theme – and in the cases of *The Visit* and *The Winter's Tale*
around an existing text – through months of argument,
rehearsal and research. An idea may germinate from
objects idly found: a cache of flowery bathing hats in
Brick Lane market led eventually to *Put It On Your Head*

(1983), 'a show about the English seaside' and the social agonies of Englishness on the beach; or it may grow from personal experience, like grief for the death of McBurney's father, after which the Company collected 'death objects' for months and came up with *A Minute Too Late* (1984) which even they, at a safe distance of several exorcising years, now call their 'smash hit show about death'.

More Bigger Snacks Now (1985) was born in the Limehouse days when McBurney, Neil Bartlett and other melancholy, unemployed actors had sifted broken dreams round an electric fire and consoling records of Callas in Bellini's *Norma*; while *Please Please Please* (1986), in which unspeakable things were done with food and an eiderdown by a birdlike old couple at Christmas, began, says McBurney, as 'a show about love, then sex, then the family, then hate'. *Please* had the lot.

In 1988, with Friedrich Dürrenmatt's *The Visit*, a revenger's comedy and masterpiece of post-war European theatre, they tackled the finite text of an established writer for the first time. It was an inspired choice. *The Visit* is also a comedy of survival, the survival of the bourgeoisie who come through on reserves of infinite corruptibility rather than the energies of desperation that inspire the working class. Complicite's total respect for it was almost as startling as the violent physical language which they developed to visualise and reinforce its harsh, ironic power.

Complicite lived with the play, on and off, for more than three years, modifying, changing and intensifying their dark comic vision of it with each revival, just as material is added to their wholly devised shows from all manner of sources in a kind of theatrical collage.

The Street of Crocodiles (1992), a narrative of missionary disruptiveness, wit and power, was assembled from the life and irrepressible writings of the Polish Jew Bruno Schulz, whom the Holocaust swept away. It took them up another notch and, with *The Three Lives of Lucie Cabrol* (1994) and *Out of a House Walked a Man* . . . (1994) – shows developed respectively from the writings of John Berger and the Russian Daniil Kharms – out into the wider world. The zealots arrived in the major touring theatres and in London's West End.

Everything Complicite actors do is rooted in what they have heard and seen. This is a theatre of bodily functions and impulses, of class-defences and universal desires. Its logic is merciless, its techniques virtuoso, its energy without bounds. It is rude and funny and fearful, for inside the vortex of frenzy the individual is always alone.

Jean in the original 1994 production

The Three Lives of
Lucie Cabrol

The Three Lives of Lucie Cabrol was first performed at The Dancehouse, Manchester, on 12 January 1994 with the following cast:

Lucie Cabrol, *the Cocadrille*	Lilo Baur
Jean	Simon McBurney
Marius Cabrol	Hannes Flaschberger
Mélanie Cabrol	Hélène Patarôt
Émile Cabrol/St Just	Stefan Metz
Henri Cabrol	Tim McMullan
Edmond Cabrol/André Masson	Mick Barnfather

Director Simon McBurney
Assistant Director Mark Wheatley
Designer Tim Hatley
Lighting Designer Paule Constable
Sound Designer Christopher Shutt
Producer Catherine Reiser
Associate Collaborators Annabel Arden
                         Annie Castledine

The Company also play the land, animals, children, villagers, and the dead. Some of the text was spoken in the actors' native languages where this was not English.

For the 1995 tours to the regions in the UK, to Europe, South Africa, Japan and Australia, the parts of La Mélanie and Henri Cabrol were taken over by Christine Marx and Paul Hamilton.

Theatre de Complicite gratefully acknowledges financial support from the Arts Council of England and London Arts Board.

Part One

Prologue

Music. The stage is covered in earth. All sit upstage except
Jean. *In front of them pairs of boots irregularly placed.*
Running water, stage left. **Jean** *enters. He washes, drinks a*
little, and comes down centre.

Jean (*indicating a pair of boots*) Émile Cabrol, who died
of his war wounds nearly twenty years after the Great
War. Émile. Eldest son of (*Indicating another pair of boots.*)
Marius Cabrol and his wife La Mélanie. (*Another pair.*)
Henri Cabrol, second son of Marius and La Mélanie,
who was to say of his sister, 'This woman has never
brought anything but shame on my family.' (*Another
pair.*) My schoolteacher, André Masson, killed at
Verdun. (*He gestures towards other pairs.*) Joset. St Just,
the maquisard. Georges, who electrocuted himself
because he knew he would become a pauper. The dead
surround the living, and the living form the core of the
dead.

Villager 1 (*sings through a makeshift loud-hailer*)
   Like a trout
   our mountain basks
   in the setting sun

   as the light drains
   the trout dies
   its mouth open

   the night
   with its wings of spruce
   flies the mountain

to the dead
to the dead
Ave Maria
Ave Maria

*All come forward and put on their boots. They lift a tin bath
and circle in a funeral procession.* **Jean** *sits at his stove.*

Jean Before I was six, perhaps I was only two or
three, I would collect the sticks for my father on winter
mornings when it was still as dark as night. We knelt
by an iron beast, feeding it. Now when I light the stove
in the morning, I say to myself: I and the fire are the
only living things in this house; my father, mother,
brothers, sisters, the horse, cows, rabbits, chickens, all
have gone. And Lucie Cabrol, who was known as the
Cocadrille, is dead.

With a crash like thunder, **Lucie** *is rolled out of her coffin and
squats silent.*

1   Birth

Jean The Cocadrille was born in 1900. 1900 . . .

All take off their outer clothes to reveal the clothes of 1900.
Marius *harnesses up his horse and begins ploughing.*

Jean The Cabrol farm is on a slope above our village
which is called Brine.

Marius *ploughs and then begins turning over the earth by hand.*

Marius That day white cloud, like smoke, was
blowing through the open door of the stable. Marius
Cabrol was milking.

La Mélanie *and* **Émile** *are revealed in turn.*

La Mélanie His wife . . .

Marius (*pointing her out*) La Mélanie.

La Mélanie . . . was in bed, on the other side of the stable wall, attended by her sister and a neighbour.

Émile Their first child had been a boy, christened Émile.

Marius Marius hoped that his second child would also be a boy and he would name him Henri after his grandfather.

La Mélanie The baby was born very quickly.

Jean *scatters a bucket of potatoes. All gather as if at the stable door.*

Marius It's a girl.

La Mélanie Jesus, forgive me! She's marked with the mark of the craving.

Villager 1 She is. It's red. It's burning.

La Mélanie She is. It's a mark. I've been punished. I've marked her.

Villager 2 Calm down, La Mélanie. It's where her face rubbed when she came out.

La Mélanie I've been punished.

Marius Stop it, woman. It's nothing. It'll be gone in a few weeks.

Pause.

Villager 1 She's a dwarf.

Villager 2 She's minute.

Marius She's tiny.

Villager 3 She's like a dwarf but she's not.

Villager 1 If she's like a dwarf, she must be a dwarf.

La Mélanie She's like a little red radish.

Marius *takes the mark from* **Lucie**'s *face.*

Marius In a few days the red mark did disappear.

La Mélanie But La Mélanie thought she had been marked in another way.

Lucie *runs off.*

You lose her as easily as you lose a button.

Villager 3 *sings a work song. All begin picking potatoes.*
Lucie *runs in grabbing at a pig.*

Lucie Soyley, soyley! Papa! The pig, the pig, the pig!

All seize the pig and take it squealing to the bathtub where it is slaughtered. **Villager 3** *cuts its throat. The men butcher it, keeping* **Lucie** *away.*

Marius Lucie, Lucie. (*He gives her the pig's tail.*)

The women take buckets of offal to the other side of the stage where they pour it all into one to clean it and make blood sausage.

La Mélanie (*to* **Lucie**) You see, nothing's wasted in a pig. Pick that up, there . . . To make the best black pudding you have to clean it properly, get rid of all the muck, see? (*She demonstrates cleaning the intestine.*) Look at that, it's a lot bigger than last year . . .

Lucie *pulls at a piece of the intestine, playing with it like rubber.*

La Mélanie Leave it alone! Go and empty the buckets!

The men go to the back where they stretch the pig's skin, a leather jacket, over two sticks. **Lucie** *plays and talks to the pig's tail. The school bell sounds, softly at first (sound made by striking the milk churn).*

Lucie (*to the dead pig*) What are you doing? What are you doing in there? You're quiet now. You're quiet now because soon you're going to be bacon!

Pig sits up in the bath, dripping wet. He gets out and becomes
Henri.

Henri Soon after Lucie was born, La Mélanie did
have another child – a boy and he *was* christened
Henri, after his grandfather.

He puts his shirt and braces on.

By the time he was two he was already bigger than his
sister. (*To* **Lucie**.) Give me that pig's tail. Go on, give it
to me.

He takes the bucket **Lucie** *is carrying and throws it to another
of the children. They tease her.*

Children Lucie, Lucie . . . ! Here, Lucie . . . !

*She can't get it back. They go into the classroom and sit on their
buckets for chairs. She follows, last, having retrieved her bucket
from the corner where it was thrown.*

2 The naming of the Cocadrille

Masson *teaches his class.*

Masson Bonjour, class.

Children Bonjour Monsieur Masson.

Masson *writes on the board.*

Children Wednesday September the tenth, nineteen
ten . . . o-ten . . .

Jean Ten!

Masson Now, the catechism. What is avarice? Joset,
let's give someone else a chance. Jean. Avarice, please!

Jean Me, Monsieur Masson? Oh . . . Avarice is –
Avarice is –

Masson Avarice is. Good, let's start there, shall we!

Jean Avarice is –

Joset (*whisper*) A big mountain!

Jean No, it's . . . it's a . . .

Lucie Avarice is an excessive longing for the good things of life especially money.

Masson Good, Lucie. And is the love of the good things of life ever justified?

Lucie Always. When it inspires thrift and foresight.

Masson Good. *Only* when it inspires thrift and foresight. Now, were we all listening?

Children Avarice is an excessive longing for the good things of life especially money . . . especially money . . . especially money . . .

They repeat it more and more softly until only **Lucie**'s *voice is heard, as we go into a work scene with the family and villagers.*

Lucie Love of the good things of life is justified only when it inspires thrift and foresight.

Henri *holds his bucket above* **Lucie**'s *head.*

Henri Henri hated his sister.

He brings it crashing down as **Lucie** *runs to work with her father.* **Marius** *chops wood on a block down left.* **Lucie** *chops beside him. Two other villagers bring up the wood.* **Marius** *sees* **Henri** *not working.*

Marius Henri. Work.

Henri *crouches beside his sister and picks up the wood she has chopped.*

Henri Do all these bits again. They should be like this, see? (*Picking up a potato.*) I'm going to do this potato. Then I'm going to do your leg. (*He chops the potato.*)

La Mélanie *goes off and returns after a moment, calling to* **Marius**.

La Mélanie   Marius! Marius! Three of my rabbits are dead.

Marius   What was it – a weasel?

La Mélanie   No. There's not a mark on them.

Marius   A fox?

La Mélanie   No, it wasn't a fox.

Marius   What was it then?

Henri   Lucie killed them.

Lucie   I didn't touch them.

Henri   She did. She looked at them and they died.

All laugh and go back to work.

She did, she did. She looked at them and they died. She's a cocadrille. That's what a cocadrille is. She can kill things by looking at them. She was born in a dung heap and she smells. She's a cocadrille.

Lucie   I'm not.

Henri   She's a cocadrille. She's a cocadrille.

Lucie   I'm not.

Henri *threatens her with a stick*.

Henri   Let's play Cocadrilles. Say you're a cocadrille.

He beats his stick around her. Then he hits the bucket she is carrying.

Say it. Say it! You're a cocadrille. Say it!

Lucie *leaps at him. They fight.* **Marius** *and* **La Mélanie** *shout at their children and then have to separate them.* **La Mélanie** *gives* **Lucie** *a postcard.*

La Mélanie Lucie, read this for me. Go on . . .

Lucie (*reading*) 'I am coming home. Émile.'

La Mélanie When?

Lucie Friday.

La Mélanie Friday.

School bell begins to sound.

Lucie Émile. Émile is coming home from Paris.

Jean *looks over her shoulder.*

Jean Émile Cabrol.

All form class again on their buckets.

Masson Bonjour, class.

Children Bonjour Monsieur Masson.

Masson Lucie, take your place. Thank you.

Lucie *sits.* **Masson** *writes on the board.*

Children Friday September the fourteenth, nineteen twelve.

Henri *spits at* **Lucie** *and taunts her.*

Masson Something to say, Henri?

Henri Lucie was born in a dung heap. She's a cocadrille. She can kill anything she looks at. She comes from a cock's egg. That's what a cocadrille is. She killed a badger on the road the other day.

Masson *begins writing on the board.*

Masson Insults!

Children read what he has written.

Children Insults should be written on sand.

Masson Compliments, Henri . . .

Children Compliments should be inscribed on marble.

Lucie *runs out.* **Masson** *calls after her.*

Masson Lucie. Lucie! Lucie!

His calls crossfade with **Émile***'s in the distance.*

Émile Lucie! Lucie!

Lucie *stands centre.* **Émile** *changes his costume in the class. He climbs. He teases her by stopping. She yells at him.*

Lucie Émile! É-mile! Did you see it?

Émile What?

Lucie The Eiffel Tower.

Émile You see it everywhere. It's more than three hundred metres high.

They continue calling, getting nearer until **Lucie** *jumps into his arms. The class has dissolved.* **Marius** *and* **La Mélanie** *greet* **Émile***.* **Henri** *sits.*

Marius (*not knowing what to say*) Good. Paris. Snow came early this year.

La Mélanie Oh, enough! Leave him alone. (*To* **Émile***.*) Take your coat off. Sit down. Eat. What did you eat in Paris? Not much, eh?

She brings **Émile** *to the table. He plays with* **Lucie** *and* **Henri***. He eats in silence. They watch.*

Émile This bread. Shepherd's bread. You never get bread like this in Paris. (*To* **Henri***.*) Do you know how many horses there are in Paris?

Lucie Three hundred and seventy-one.

Émile Two million.

Marius *cuffs him on the head.*

Marius (*derisively*) Two million. Two million! (*Laughing.*) That's a lot of shit!

Goes back to his work.

Émile (*to the others*) In Paris there is a metro too. The metro is a train that goes underground. Parisians are lazy – they can't get out of bed in the mornings. You should see them running along the tunnels to catch their trains. (*Looking at* **Henri***, he puts a silver-painted model of the Eiffel Tower in front of* **Lucie**.) On a clear night you can see more lights in the city than there are stars in the sky.

Lucie Did you climb to the top?

Émile What top?

Lucie The top of the Eiffel Tower!

Émile You go up by lift.

Lucie Lift?

Émile Yes, a lift.

Lucie What's lift?

The others laugh.

What's lift?

Henri The Cocadrille knows nothing! The proper place for her is her dung heap.

Lucie *gets up, finds a pail of milk, picks it up and hurls the milk into* **Henri**'s *face.*

Lucie If you weren't a weasel, I'd kill you!

La Mélanie Marius!

Marius *comes in from milking. He catches* **Lucie** *by the ear and takes her round the table to the corner. He beats her.*

Marius   Milk is not water! Milk is not water!

La Mélanie   Marius!

He stops. He strides back to his work. **Lucie** *comes over to him and watches. After a moment* **Marius** *can't ignore her. He picks her up and holds her.*

Marius   Ah, my Cocadrille! My Cocadrille. (*To* **La Mélanie**.) I know – she just came out like that, didn't she? I know she can't help it.

He pinches **Lucie**'s *cheek.*

She just came out like that. My Cocadrille. My Cocadrille! My Cocadrille! My Cocadrille!

He dances with her, spinning round and round. Then he puts her down and she runs with the other children.

Jean   And so the name Cocadrille, born of both hatred and love, replaced the name Lucie.

Children   The Cocadrille! The Cocadrille!

The children's chanting turns nasty as the school bell begins to sound.

Cocadrille! Cocadrille! Cocadrille!

They line up to form the class, which **Masson** *walks through.*

Masson   Bonjour, class.

The others sit on their buckets. **Jean** *takes* **Masson**'s *coat as he writes on the board.*

Jean   August the eleventh 1914.

Masson   André Masson was killed at Verdun. Each morning he wrote on the board the day of the week, the

date of the month and the year of the century. On the
war memorial there is only the month and the year of
his death. March 1916.

The class begin scything where they sit and slowly get up.

3   The First War and the birth of Edmond

*The family is scything on the slopes. The stick held by one
strikes the spade held by another. A tolling bell.*

Marius   The war has started.

*The family look down left as if tracing the source of the sound
in the valley below.*

La Mélanie   The massacre of the world has begun.

Marius *goes to* **La Mélanie**. *He gives her his stick which is
taken by* **Lucie**.

Marius   I'll be back before the snow. I'll be back.

He marches upstage. **Jean** *runs downstage, excited.*

Jean   Émile, Émile, I got my mobilisation papers.
They're in the village.

The others follow him, **Émile** *last. Cheers. They begin singing
as they march off to war.* **Marius** *joins the end of their
procession reluctantly.*

Men
    Oh-U, oh-U, oh-Ursula
    Pour toi d'amour mon cœur brule
    Il faudrait l'énergie d'une pompe à vapeur
    Pour éteindre le feu qui consume mon cœur

*They continue until they stand upstage. They suddenly stop
singing in mid-march. Freeze.*

La Mélanie Marius did not come back before the snow came, nor before the new year, nor before the spring. The endless time of war began.

Lucie Maman!

La Mélanie La Mélanie, the Cocadrille and Henri were left to run the farm.

Lucie *works.* **Henri** *stands on the table watching. The men resume their song faintly and march on the spot.*

La Mélanie The Cocadrille was tireless. She was not the second woman of the house, she was more like a hired hand – a man.

Lucie *drives the horse.*

Henri A midget man with a difficult and unpredictable character.

La Mélanie She drove the mare, she fetched the wood, she milked the cows, she dug the garden, she made the cider, she preserved the fruit, she mended the harnesses. But she never washed clothes nor sewed.

Henri There was so much to be done that Henri could no longer afford to quarrel openly with his sister.

Lucie *continues working. Song rises.* **Émile** *screams.*

Lucie Émile. Émile.

Lucie *rushes to buckets for milking.*

I will milk nine, no ten, buckets a day, to keep you alive. (*To the milk.*) Keep him alive. Keep Émile alive. Émile, come back. Come back. (*She prays.*) Our Father, Who art in heaven, hallowed be Thy name . . .

Émile *is carried home.* **Lucie** *looks at him and follows him. She pushes* **Henri** *off his chair and* **Émile** *is seated. She gives him soup.*

Jean No one in the village spoke of victory. They only spoke of the war being ended.

La Mélanie *waits for* **Marius**.

La Mélanie Marius. Marius!

Unseen, he watches her and walks towards her. He grabs her from behind and lifts her into the air. **Lucie** *goes to get* **Marius**'s *stick*.

Émile At her age!

Marius It will be her last.

Lucie Papa.

Lucie *gives* **Marius** *his stick and another.* *He harnesses* **La Mélanie**.

Émile It will have to be!

Marius All the war I promised myself that.

He begins ploughing.

Émile So we'll be four. The farm will be divided into four.

Henri Only if you count the Cocadrille.

Émile Oh, shut up! (*To* **Marius**.) Have you told the Cocadrille?

Marius Not yet. It's for Mother to tell her.

Émile It'll change the Cocadrille. Me and the Cocadrille, we might be married now with our own children.

Edmond *lands on* **Marius**'s *back as he ploughs*.

Émile Yet who is going to marry the Cocadrille? And I'm too sick to marry. It ought be our turn and, instead, you've made another baby.

Marius (*smiling*) Call it an old man's last sin!

Marius *turns and goes upstage.* **Edmond** *drops centre and stands beside* **Henri**.

Edmond In September 1919 La Mélanie had her fourth child, a boy, who was christened . . .

Henri *gives him a lit cigarette. He takes a puff.*

. . . Edmond.

4   The mountain pastures

Jean *comes from upstage.*

Jean Now, every summer the village took all the cattle up to the mountain pastures, the alpage.

The sound of the cows and goats.

Up there it was mostly the young women who looked after the cows and goats.

The young men get ready to climb the mountain. They strap upturned chairs to their backs for haversacks, provisions.

It was the unmarried daughter who had the pair of hands most easily spared from the work in the valley below. And from time to time a visiting priest would preach a sermon against the immorality of leaving young women alone in the alpage.

The men put on their hats.

Man 1 Joset.

Man 2 Véronique.

Man 3 Rosemarie.

Man 4 La belle Jacqueline.

Jean La Nan Bessons.

La Mélanie *stands on the table, centre.*

La Mélanie   Old women still talk of their summers in the alpage.

She comes down helped by **Men** *as they begin their 'climb' up towards the table.*

Their summers in the alpage.

Men *climb onto and over the table and back until they stand on top.*

Man 4   You can see André's sheep from here.

Man 1   He's slow is André.

Man 3   He's slowed down since the death of Honorine.

Jean   He should marry again.

All   Philomène!

They laugh. They make the sound of the birds flapping and watch them fly past. **La Mélanie** *watching down right, picks up the bird sounds and sends them back again.* **Men** *repeat the names of their women. They set out to climb again.*

Man 4   No, no, not that way. The Cocadrille has her chalet up there. We'll have to go round.

They climb and stop at a water trough down left. As they turn to go, **Lucie** *appears in front of them.* **Man 2** *is playing with his harmonica.*

Lucie   You have a harmonica.

Man 2   Yes, we have.

Lucie   I can dance.

Jean   Not in those sabots, you can't!

She kicks them off and dances, singing.

Lucie
Apricagot de lee nay-a

Sopiya-a, *etc.*
(*A mountain peasant song in a dead language.*)

The **Men** *join in.*

Jean Stop! The music will tell the other girls that we are here.

They stop.

We must go.

Lucie Can one of you help me to move a barrel?

All Go on, Georges . . .

Lucie No, not you, I want the one who has just come back from the army.

Men *laugh.*

All Go on, Jean . . . La Nan Bessons! . . .

Jean (*to the others*) You tell La Nan I'm definitely coming to visit her! Definitely!

All Definitely!

Jean *reluctantly goes to* **Lucie**. *The others laugh and go.*

Lucie Let them go.

Lucie'*s chalet is made with planks upright to one side and the table on the other. Behind the planks we hear the cows and goats crying and stamping in their stable.*

Jean (*awkwardly*) You know what they say about you in the village? They say she's so small she could get a job as a chimney sweep.

Lucie I'm a woman and I'd shit down their chimneys.

Jean Right!

Jean *begins to move the barrel, putting all his weight behind it. He discovers it is light and moves it easily.*

Lucie   Are you going away to Paris this autumn?

Jean   Yes.

She gives him a small glass and pours him some gnole. She drinks from the bottle.

Lucie   Will you go up the Eiffel Tower?

Jean   Maybe. I must be going. The others will be waiting.

Lucie   They're singing, can't you hear?

Distant harmonica.

I'll fetch you some butter.

Jean   We don't need any.

Lucie   You have so much at home that you can refuse butter?

She leaves and goes through into the stable, returning moments later. She no longer has any clothes on the upper half of her body. Her breasts are covered with milk. **Jean** *begins to run, returns for his hat, and stops. He kneels and licks the milk from her. Then he stands and runs out of the chalet and down the mountainside. His flight is made by a succession of chairs and the milk churn placed in his way. He runs over them and through them. He sits, panting.*

Jean   What was it that made me go back the following night? Why did I deliberately go up alone, avoiding my companions?

He 'climbs' back up and goes into the chalet. The sound of the animals.

Lucie   So you've finished the butter!

Jean   Can I have some more?

Lucie Yes, Jean.

*She gives **Jean** some milk and spills it down his chest. A crash of thunder. He takes off his shirt. She wipes her hand on him and licks him. They play. He lifts her. They crash into the wall of planks. And then through them. They roll back on under the planks. The planks swing above them and drop in front of them. The planks slow to a gentle swinging motion until they make a door which, after a moment, **Jean** opens. **Jean** and **Lucie** go through it and sit.*

Jean We played and made love on the wooden stage of the bed as though we possessed the strength of the whole village. But perhaps that is an old man's boast.

A stream flows down one of the planks.

Lucie So, my goat, with me you can climb.

Jean *plays the goat.*

Lucie The stars, Jean, look. They're so close, I could pick you one.

They go to the stream and drink and throw water at each other. They lie down.

When my brothers divide the farm, I'll get the slopes, the part they don't want. The steep part. Nobody'll marry me, Jean. Too steep. But you, my goat, you can climb!

Jean *lifts his head suddenly as if not sure what he's heard. Then he gets up and begins getting ready to go.*

Lucie Jean?

Jean Lucie, I'm not going to come up again.

Lucie I didn't expect you to, Jean.

Jean It wasn't true that she would never marry. She was plotting to make me her husband. She believed she was already pregnant and I would be forced to marry her.

He runs down the mountainside. This time around the space.
Until he falls onto the table and draws a blanket over him and
sleeps. After a moment, **Lucie** *rushes in and perches on the edge*
of the table bed. All join her and stand around him. His dream:

Lucie Only one man can be the father of my child and
that is you, Jean!

Father Is it true? With the Cocadrille? I don't believe
it.

Lucie I can prove it.

Father Then prove it!

Lucie I counted the moles on the small of his back.

Father How many are there?

Lucie Seven.

They pull down **Jean***'s trousers, bend him over the table, and*
count. Pause after 'six', until **Father** *triumphantly finds –*

Father Seven! You've ruined your life! Ruined it for
nothing!

They withdraw. **Marius** *appears with a pail of milk. He falls.*
The milk spills. **Jean** *wakes and screams.* **Lucie** *screams and*
runs to **Marius***.* **La Mélanie** *and the others join her and*
mourn **Marius***.*

Lucie Papa! Papa!

She prays over him. They lift him in a funeral procession.

5   Marius's funeral and Marie

Jean (*getting up and folding his blanket*) I woke up
frightened and sweating. And when I saw her again,
three months later, it was at her father's funeral. To my

relief, she was not pregnant. But by then, I had already made up my mind. I was going to leave the village. That was in the summer of 1924.

Lucie *comes to* **Jean** *from the procession.*

Lucie So you are leaving us?

Jean Yes. First to Paris. Then I'm going to South America.

Lucie Come back before you die.

She rejoins the procession which goes upstage.

Émile In 1936 Émile died as the final consequence of his war wounds.

Émile *takes off his jacket and goes to the back of the procession.*

La Mélanie Two years later La Mélanie followed her husband and her eldest son into the grave.

She puts her apron around **Lucie** *and goes to the back of the procession where she removes her top clothes to become* **Marie.** **Lucie** *stands and sharpens her scythe.*

Henri Henri, Edmond and the Cocadrille were left to run the farm.

Henri *stands opposite* **Lucie** *sharpening his scythe.*

Lucie (*to scythe*) For twenty summers I've cherished you like a son. If they gave me money, I could never find another one like you.

Henri Henri married Marie, a woman from the next village.

Cheers. Rice is thrown over **Marie** *as she is lifted onto the table with a bundle containing lunch. She comes down and hands it to* **Henri** *and* **Edmond.**

Marie Hey, here it is, lunch! And don't tell me I'm late because it's me who's done all the work again this morning. I fed the chickens, scrubbed the floor, stacked the wood. You should tell her I'm not madam's skivvy.

They sit without **Lucie**. **Lucie** *goes to join them and picks up the water and drinks.*

Lucie However much you drink when you're making hay, you never piss!

She goes back to work.

Marie She's as dirty as a chicken house. And she never lifts a finger in the kitchen. What kind of woman is that?

Henri *and* **Edmond** *go back to work. They scythe. They freeze together.*

Henri The years passed. The Second War broke out.

6   The maquisards

Henri, **Edmond** *and* **Lucie** *scything.* **Henri** *looks up and sees two men watching them.*

Peasant from the Dranse Good morning.

Henri Shit!

Edmond They're maquisards.

Henri What else could they be?

Edmond Jesus! We can't let anyone else see them.

Peasant from the Dranse Two of us need shelter for twenty-four hours.

Turns to **Lucie**.

Good morning, little girl.

She turns.

Sorry, I didn't see –

Lucie This is also my farm.

Lucie *continues to work.*

Edmond Where are you from?

Peasant from the Dranse From the Dranse. The SS burned down my father's farm there.

Henri All right, you can have some food but after that you must go.

Peasant from the Dranse No, we need to stay till tomorrow. The comrade here has a wound that needs dressing.

Henri We are not a hospital.

Lucie I can dress it for you.

Henri And if the Germans come? He can't be in the house.

Peasant from the Dranse No, he's right. Better we stay up here. (*To* **Lucie**.) Can you, madam, get some hot water and bandages. Please go, quickly.

The sound of an armoured car approaching.

Edmond They're Germans. The Germans, Henri!

Henri Work. Work! (*To the second maquisard,* **St Just**.) Take that scythe and don't look up.

The car sound gets louder. The maquisards pretend to work.

The car is now very close. It passes. **St Just** *falls.*

Henri Get up. Work!

Peasant from the Dranse Leave him!

Lucie It's safe now. They won't come back. (*To* **St Just**.) You can go and rest in the hayloft.

Henri And if they come back and find him!

Lucie If they come back he can pretend to be working.

Henri And if he's asleep?

Lucie I'll stay with him.

Henri Stay with him! You'll stay here and get this hay in.

Lucie *wheels the wheelbarrow downstage.* **Henri** *stops her, banging the stick of his scythe into the front of the barrow.*

It's not your farm they'll burn down. It's mine!

A stand-off. Moments pass. **Lucie** *looks at him.* **Henri** *moves away.* **Lucie** *helps* **St Just** *into the barrow and wheels him round and back downstage.* **The Peasant from the Dranse** *goes with them and keeps guard. Lighting changes to barn.* **Lucie** *undresses* **St Just** *and begins bathing his wound.*

Lucie What is your first name?

St Just They call me St Just.

Lucie I have never heard that name. Rest now, St Just.

St Just You have very gentle hands.

Lucie Gentle! They've been in too much shit to be gentle. How old are you?

St Just Nineteen.

Peasant from the Dranse The wound near the top of his thigh was like a wound of any generation. It was as red as raw beef.

Lucie Is your father still alive.

St Just He is a judge.

Lucie You died, Papa, not knowing that to make a child you need a woman, a man and the devil!

Henri, **Marie** *and* **Edmond** *are seated at the table.*

Henri The mayor was reluctant to refer the arson of the Cabrol barn to any outside authority.

Marie It was the mayor's wife who came up with the solution which he finally proposed to Henri and Edmond. They accepted it enthusiastically.

Edmond *comes round the table, sweeps the debris from it and sits in* **Lucie**'s *place.*

Marie And with this proposal the first life of the Cocadrille came to an end.

Lucie *walks. She is loaded up with possessions – a sack, a spade, a chair, a blanket, her scythe – until she is bent under their weight. She circles the space and goes off up right. Fade.*

Lucie What will you do when the war stops?

St Just I will continue my studies.

Lucie And one day become a judge like your father?

St Just No, it is another kind of justice that I believe in, a popular justice, a justice for peasants like you and for workers . . .

Lucie *squeezes a bloody sponge onto his bare thigh.*

. . . A justice which gives factories to those who work in them, and the land to those who cultivate it.

Lucie Is your father rich?

St Just Fairly.

Lucie Won't you inherit some of his money one day?

St Just All of it when he dies.

Lucie There's the difference between us.

St Just I shall use the money to start a paper. By then we shall have a free press. A free press is a prerequisite for the full mobilisation of the masses.

Lucie (*taking off her shoes*) Really? Are *your* feet hot too?

St Just (*laughing*) The hay is dusty.

Lucie Meanwhile you are in danger.

St Just Not more than you.

Lucie That is true. Today we are equal.

St Just Your brothers – do they think like you?

Lucie I don't think.

St Just I didn't trust them.

Lucie They are as straight as a goat's hind leg. You must rest now . . . St Just.

She gives him something to drink.

St Just I feel much stronger. Sit beside me . . . please.

She sits with him. He lays his head in her lap. She strokes his hair.

You have very gentle hands.

Lucie It's like raking hay!

The Peasant from the Dranse *lifts* **St Just** *and they stand together.*

Peasant from the Dranse The two maquisards left the next day. Within forty-eight hours the village heard that a group of maquisards had been surprised in their camp, taken prisoner and shot.

Henri *comes forward to chop wood.*

Henri Within forty-eight hours the village heard that a group of maquisards had been surprised in their camp by the milice, taken into the fields and shot. It was said that they would never have been found unless they had been tipped off by an informer.

He chops wood. Blood is thrown on **St Just**. **Lucie** *screams. She throws the wheelbarrow over. She puts* **St Just**'s *cartridge belt over her head and runs, carrying the rest of his clothes.*

7   The casting out

Henri, **Edmond** *and* **Marie** *sit and eat.* **Lucie** *enters sobbing.*

Marie She's as dirty as a chicken house. And she never lifts a finger in the kitchen. What kind of woman is that? In God's name, stop it woman! A woman of your age should be ashamed!

Edmond Those who sleep with dogs, wake up with fleas!

Henri (*lighting a cigarette*) That's good! Th sleep with dogs, wake up with fleas!

Lucie *goes. She chops wood, brings it back and onto each of their plates. She empties a bucket of the table. She mimics ploughing with the harness throws them onto the table. She picks up a bucket*

Lucie No. No!

And pours it away. She throws the milk churn off she curses them and sobs. She crouches down left. sniffing suspiciously and then discovers the red of them.

Henri Fire. Fire in the barn!

The noise of a large fire. Its red glow. **Edmond** *leap up from the table. All beat out the fire.* **Hen** *forward.*

Henri This woman has never brought any shame on my family.

Lucie *prays.*

Lucie Maman. Papa. You should have kn sons better.

Henri She started by stealing from us. No from our neighbours.

Lucie You always thought of them as they they were in the cradle.

Henri She never does any work any more

Lucie Shit! You didn't know where their from.

Henri If she lived in a city, she'd have be institution years ago!

Lucie What will you do when the war stops?

St Just I will continue my studies.

Lucie And one day become a judge like your father?

St Just No, it is another kind of justice that I believe in, a popular justice, a justice for peasants like you and for workers . . .

Lucie *squeezes a bloody sponge onto his bare thigh.*

. . . A justice which gives factories to those who work in them, and the land to those who cultivate it.

Lucie Is your father rich?

St Just Fairly.

Lucie Won't you inherit some of his money one day?

St Just All of it when he dies.

Lucie There's the difference between us.

St Just I shall use the money to start a paper. By then we shall have a free press. A free press is a prerequisite for the full mobilisation of the masses.

Lucie (*taking off her shoes*) Really? Are *your* feet hot too?

St Just (*laughing*) The hay is dusty.

Lucie Meanwhile you are in danger.

St Just Not more than you.

Lucie That is true. Today we are equal.

St Just Your brothers – do they think like you?

Lucie I don't think.

St Just I didn't trust them.

Lucie They are as straight as a goat's hind leg. You must rest now . . . St Just.

She gives him something to drink.

St Just I feel much stronger. Sit beside me . . . please.

She sits with him. He lays his head in her lap. She strokes his hair.

You have very gentle hands.

Lucie It's like raking hay!

The Peasant from the Dranse *lifts* **St Just** *and they stand together.*

Peasant from the Dranse The two maquisards left the next day. Within forty-eight hours the village heard that a group of maquisards had been surprised in their camp, taken prisoner and shot.

Henri *comes forward to chop wood.*

Henri Within forty-eight hours the village heard that a group of maquisards had been surprised in their camp by the milice, taken into the fields and shot. It was said that they would never have been found unless they had been tipped off by an informer.

He chops wood. Blood is thrown on **St Just**. **Lucie** *screams. She throws the wheelbarrow over. She puts* **St Just**'s *cartridge belt over her head and runs, carrying the rest of his clothes.*

7   The casting out

Henri, **Edmond** *and* **Marie** *sit and eat.* **Lucie** *enters sobbing.*

Marie She's as dirty as a chicken house. And she never lifts a finger in the kitchen. What kind of woman is that? In God's name, stop it woman! A woman of your age should be ashamed!

Edmond Those who sleep with dogs, wake up with fleas!

Henri (*lighting a cigarette*) That's good! Those who sleep with dogs, wake up with fleas!

Lucie *goes. She chops wood, brings it back and bangs a piece onto each of their plates. She empties a bucket of potatoes onto the table. She mimics ploughing with the harness sticks and throws them onto the table. She picks up a bucket of milk.*

Lucie No. No!

And pours it away. She throws the milk churn off. All the while she curses them and sobs. She crouches down left. **Henri** *begins sniffing suspiciously and then discovers the red of a fire beneath them.*

Henri Fire. Fire in the barn!

The noise of a large fire. Its red glow. **Edmond** *and* **Marie** *leap up from the table. All beat out the fire.* **Henri** *comes forward.*

Henri This woman has never brought anything but shame on my family.

Lucie *prays.*

Lucie Maman. Papa. You should have known your sons better.

Henri She started by stealing from us. Now she steals from our neighbours.

Lucie You always thought of them as they were when they were in the cradle.

Henri She never does any work any more.

Lucie Shit! You didn't know where their evil came from.

Henri If she lived in a city, she'd have been put in an institution years ago!

Lucie You died, Papa, not knowing th
child you need a woman, a man and th

Henri, **Marie** *and* **Edmond** *are seated* a

Henri The mayor was reluctant to r
the Cabrol barn to any outside autho

Marie It was the mayor's wife who
solution which he finally proposed to
Edmond. They accepted it enthusia

Edmond *comes round the table, sweeps*
sits in **Lucie**'s *place.*

Marie And with this proposal the
Cocadrille came to an end.

Lucie *walks. She is loaded up with p*
spade, a chair, a blanket, her scythe —
their weight. She circles the space and

Henri (*lighting a cigarette*) That's good! Those who sleep with dogs, wake up with fleas!

Lucie *goes. She chops wood, brings it back and bangs a piece onto each of their plates. She empties a bucket of potatoes onto the table. She mimics ploughing with the harness sticks and throws them onto the table. She picks up a bucket of milk.*

Lucie No. No!

And pours it away. She throws the milk churn off. All the while she curses them and sobs. She crouches down left. **Henri** *begins sniffing suspiciously and then discovers the red of a fire beneath them.*

Henri Fire. Fire in the barn!

The noise of a large fire. Its red glow. **Edmond** *and* **Marie** *leap up from the table. All beat out the fire.* **Henri** *comes forward.*

Henri This woman has never brought anything but shame on my family.

Lucie *prays.*

Lucie Maman. Papa. You should have known your sons better.

Henri She started by stealing from us. Now she steals from our neighbours.

Lucie You always thought of them as they were when they were in the cradle.

Henri She never does any work any more.

Lucie Shit! You didn't know where their evil came from.

Henri If she lived in a city, she'd have been put in an institution years ago!

Lucie You died, Papa, not knowing that to make a child you need a woman, a man and the devil!

Henri, **Marie** and **Edmond** *are seated at the table.*

Henri The mayor was reluctant to refer the arson of the Cabrol barn to any outside authority.

Marie It was the mayor's wife who came up with the solution which he finally proposed to Henri and Edmond. They accepted it enthusiastically.

Edmond *comes round the table, sweeps the debris from it and sits in* **Lucie**'s *place.*

Marie And with this proposal the first life of the Cocadrille came to an end.

Lucie *walks. She is loaded up with possessions – a sack, a spade, a chair, a blanket, her scythe – until she is bent under their weight. She circles the space and goes off up right. Fade.*

Part Two

8   Jean's return (forty years later)

Sound of the wind. All sit upstage. **Lucie** *enters with a sack. She takes out a Marlboro and smokes.* **Jean** *enters with haversack. He watches her through binoculars.* **Lucie** *begins picking. The others come forward and make the bushes.*

Jean   In the hot airless nights in Buenos Aires, when I lived on the fourteenth floor, not far from one of the worst shanty towns in the city, I used to stand at my window and dream of an alpine summer. After twenty-five years in the Argentine, I went north to Montreal where I had a bar and for a while, I was rich. Since my return I had only heard of the Cocadrille from others.

Lucie *squats to shit and sees him.*

Lucie   The passer-by should always raise his hat to the one who is shitting!

Jean *takes off his beret. She laughs and comes towards him.*

It's Jean! Do you recognise me?

Jean   You're the Cocadrille.

Lucie   No! Why are you following me?

Jean   I came up here to look for mushrooms, for bolets.

Lucie   You found some?

Jean   What?

Lucie   Did you find some?

Jean   Yes.

Lucie   Give them to me.

Jean What for?

Lucie They are mine!

He closes his sack. She turns away, muttering.

So you've come back.

Jean Yes, I've come back.

Lucie (*staring at him*) You were away too long.

Jean I remembered the way up here.

Lucie You came up here to spy on me.

Jean Spy?

Lucie Spy on me!

Jean Why should I want to spy on you?

Lucie Give me the bolets then.

Jean No. They're mine.

She curses him and continues picking raspberries.

Lucie Whilst you were away, everything changed.

Jean I suppose a lot must have changed when you left the farm.

Lucie I didn't leave it. They threw me out. Did you marry out there?

Jean Yes, I did.

Lucie Why did you come back alone then?

Jean Because my wife died.

Lucie *crosses herself.*

Lucie Oh. You're a widower.

Jean I am a widower.

Lucie Do you have children?

Jean Two boys. They are both working in the United States.

Lucie America. America. Money can change everything. Money can eat and dance. Money can make the dirty clean. Money can make the dwarf big. I have two million!

Jean I hope you keep it in a bank!

Lucie Fuck off! Fuck off and get away!

She strides off, taking his haversack with her. The bushes now become a flock of birds disturbed by her. They squawk and fly off.

Jean Wait! I need my haversack!

Lucie You know where I live!

9 Lucie's hut

Jean Half an hour's walk east of the village brings you to a stone column on top of which stands a small statue of the Madonna. Around the next corner, sitting on a bend in the road, sheltered under a precipice, is the house in which the Cocadrille lived her second life.

He stands outside her hut. The table is its door. He knocks.

Lucie You're too late.

Jean I have come to fetch my haversack.

Lucie At this hour!

Jean I won't come in.

The table goes back to reveal her.

Lucie All right, I'll pay you a coffee.

*He goes in and sits. She cuts newspaper with a knife. The sound
of chickens picking around the hut. The others, a chorus of the
dead, listen at* **Lucie***'s door.*

Jean   What are you doing?

Lucie   Something to wipe my arse with! Take your
glasses off, they make you look like a priest. The last
visitor I had was the priest. That was three years ago.
In July 1964. It was the last priest, not this one. He'd
climbed up here on his way somewhere in his cassock
and his little pompom. He was always in bad health. I
could hear him coming for miles, wheezing and
coughing. He asked for a glass of water but I knew
what he needed – some gnole.

*A chicken wearing a priest's biretta has settled on a chair behind
her.*

Cock   You are a child of the earth, Lucie.

Lucie   He said. Without land, I said.

Cock   You have things to be grateful for.

Lucie   Like this house you mean. Oh yes. Everybody
whispers in the village that I don't pay rent for it. But
look what a shack it is. It was built for one man and a
horse. It was built for the roadmender. I'm the first
woman who ever slept in this house. Name me another
woman, I said, who would live up here.

Cock   None of them is a child of the earth, Lucie.

Lucie   I will show you one day what I am. I'm going
to surprise you all. Father, I believe in happiness. (*She
shoos away the cock.*) That was the last visitor I had.
Where do you live?

Jean   In my mother's house in the village. I bought it
from my brothers with money when I had it.

Lucie So you have money?

Jean I didn't make the fortune I dreamed of . . .

Lucie That's obvious.

Jean I was unlucky. Do you always sit in the dark?

Lucie What did you find in South America – electricity?

Jean A little more.

Lucie What?

Jean Enough to live on until they nail me in my coffin.

Lucie So you've come back to die?

Jean We're not young any more.

Lucie I'm not ready to die yet.

Jean Death doesn't ask if you are ready.

Lucie If death comes to my door I'll tell him I'm not ready. I'm not ready!

The chorus of the dead at her door recoil a little. **Lucie** *chatters quickly and unintelligibly to herself. And stops, embarrassed.*

Were you unfaithful to your wife?

Jean (*standing*) What a man does with his own skin is his own business. I'll take my haversack and I'll be going.

Lucie *fixes him with her look.* **Jean** *is made to sit down again.*

Lucie All right, I'll heat the soup.

Jean All right, then. I have a bottle of wine. (*Taking it from his haversack.*)

Lucie So you thought you'd stay!

Jean No. I bought it for myself at home. But we might as well have it now.

Lucie After forty years that's all you have to show for
it. One litre of red. (*To the stove.*) Did you hear that?
He's come back a pauper. At least he's seen the world.
(*To* **Jean**.) You went round the world and I kept myself
and here I am, Jean. I kept myself together. Waiting.
Forty years I kept them off. Keeping myself, waiting.
When you left and they threw me into this hut of
stones, I looked at my hands – you can look at them,
too.

Jean *stands and backs away down left where he sits to listen to
her story. The hut expands to fill the space.*

Poor hands, I said, all your life you have worked and
what can you do now in this hut of stones?

The chorus raise the Madonna.

No land, no cow to milk, no pig to feed, no field to cut.
I looked at my hands and then I looked at the hands of
the Madonna – you know the one who stands on her
column by the road through the rocks – and they are
the same hands, Jean.

Lucie *has come centre to look.*

And I looked and I saw where her hands were pointing
in the grass at my feet, and there was a morille. And
another. And another. A bed full of mushrooms. I
picked and picked and put them in my skirt. In no time
I had two kilos in there.

The Madonna disappears.

Too many for any plate of mine. And I heard Father
saying –

Marius *appears from behind the table.*

Marius Lucie, in the city you can buy anything if you
have money. In the city money breeds. Buy, sell, buy,
sell, buy, sell. And it makes little money and when little

money gets big and fat you kill it. In the city you can make money with nothing. (*He spits.*)

Lucie Yes, Papa. So I went to the city. With my skirt full of mushrooms. I took the train, I crossed the frontier, I walked for three hours and I thought, I can make 2000 with a skirt full of mushrooms. And then I saw the prices.

The chorus come forward as market traders, shouting their wares, competing.

7000 for one kilo! 7000! Yes, Papa, in the city money breeds.

The chorus retreat and fade.

All around me people were buying and selling and I was just sitting and waiting. Waiting for people to buy my mushrooms. But nobody bought. And then at twelve everyone started to pack up and leave. I hadn't sold anything. I hadn't opened my mouth. In the city you have to know what they want and how to sell it. Cèpes! Morilles! Bluettes! Pigs' feet. Ox tongues. Monks' noses. Wolves' balls. Death's trumpets – all the mushrooms, Jean. I still know where a mushroom is waiting like a bitch on heat for a dog. And if they want raspberries, I pick the wild raspberries. In the autumn it's the blackberries. In the summer it's the blueberries. And then the redberries, the huckleberries, the juniper berries, the gooseberries, the bilberries and the whateverberries. (*Going back to her table down right.*) And at Christmas, for a bunch of mistletoe, I even get 5000.

Sound of a car passing, the headlights shine into her face.
Lucie *raises her fist and swears at it.*

They never stop. In the winter when they go past, I think of shooting the driver. Why not! In the winter it's only the three of us. The two needles and me. (*She finds them behind her*.) But we work together. We knit little ski caps, gloves, and baby boots. But we have to know who to knit for. If we sell them in the market we get 2000. If we go to the wool shop we get 3500. You have to know where to sell. Next to the wool shop there's a shop window full of wood. Old wood. Things we have in our barns – our hayforks, sledges, cradles, milking stools . . .

Jean   Antiques, I think they call them.

Lucie   Antique, antique! I went in this antique once and I said, if a stool costs that much how much would I cost. I could sell myself, piece by piece. 20,000 for a milking hand. Double that for an arm. And how much would you give, I asked, for a real peasant woman's arsehole? It's still working, this one, even if it is an antique! In the city you can make money with nothing.

She goes to **Jean**.

Do you still drink gnole? (*She pours him some.*) You know how much I sell a bottle of this for? Eh? Eh? 9000. Don't think me a fool, Jean – I found out about Marlboro. Marlboro. 2000 in the city.

She crosses the frontier, made by the customs officer.

Customs officer   Anything to declare, grandma?

Lucie   No. (*To* **Jean**.) I sell them for 3000 this side of the frontier. I'm a smuggler!

She goes back to her table where she picks up her bag and hat to go shopping.

Yes, everything in the city is hidden. Everything is arranged in private. Private cars, private houses, private restaurants. It took me two years to find my way around and even after two years there were things I didn't know. One day it was raining and I was caught

in a crowd. I found myself pushed into a huge shop. I'd
never been in this shop. How did I miss such a big
one? I said to myself. And there I was, standing in
front of a lift. Émile! If only you could see me now!

Lift operator Chocolate, coffee, teas, patisseries.
Madame?

*She sits in a café. The chorus of the dead are the other
customers. Two men meet and talk behind, and a man and a
woman to her left.* **Lucie** *is served tea.*

Lucie For eighteen years that was the only day of the
week I sat in company. (*She smokes. She imitates the
laughter of the woman at the next table.*) Me with my
Marlboro and them with their new shoes. This is what
money can do.

The man and woman get up to leave. **Lucie** *stops the woman.*

Hey. If you have enough money you can stand on your
head stark naked.

She laughs. The man puts a coin in her cup. She spits.

I have enough. I have enough.

*She wraps her small box-table into the cloth and takes it back to
the table in the hut as if it were her savings. Café fades.*

I have enough. I brought back money. And money
saves you. Money keeps you. I kept myself. You're a
pauper, Jean. Not me. My savings talk to me. When
I'm soaked in the forest, they say –

The dead advance and speak to her like her savings.

Savings One day, Lucie, you'll be warm and dry.

Lucie When my back feels broken, they say –

Savings One day you'll have an armchair.

Lucie And when I'm sick of talking to myself, they
say:

Savings One day, Lucie, you'll move back into the village.

Chorus The village, the village . . .

Lucie That's what my savings say. Why don't you say something? What did you lose on your travels – your tongue? Why don't you say something, Jean?

Jean Haven't your brothers, Henri and Edmond, ever visited you?

Lucie I saw the last of them the same night they brought my furniture up here. My own brothers, fed on the same mother's milk left me up here in the dark one night. Each month they were meant to pay me. Pay my arse! I watched them go through that window there. I followed them as far as the Madonna.

Chorus raise the Madonna.

There was a long white cloud in the shape of a fish. And where the fish's eye should have been was the moon. (**Lucie** *prays to the Madonna.*) Papa. Maman. You should have known your sons better. You always thought of them as they were when they were in the cradle. Shit! You didn't know where their evil came from. You died, Papa, not knowing that to make a child you need a woman, a man and the devil. That's why it's so tempting. (*She sees her mother and father.*) Papa, Maman. Go on, Papa, rut into Maman. Maman, pull him down! Go on, Papa, rut into Maman. When you were alive, you didn't do it enough, did you, you were always too tired and your back felt too broken. I give you my blessing. You have nothing left here. (*She turns to the Madonna again.*) If you stopped and saw me, you'd suffer. I'm not going to let you suffer, Papa, I'm not going to let you suffer, Maman, because I'm going to survive. I swear it. I'm not going to let you suffer.

I'm going to survive. (*Going back to her table*.) And I have survived. My savings get me out of bed every morning before sunrise.

Chorus follow her.

They remind me when my dress is wet with dew that it will dry in an hour.

Crack of a bamboo whip behind her.

They tell me not to complain when I'm hungry because I'll eat later. (*The whip*.) And when my back aches and my shoulders are sore and my knees give me so much pain they make me cry out, (*The whip*.) they remind me that one day I will buy a new bed and that I will move back into the village. (*The whip cracks again*.)

Jean   Why are you telling me all this?

Lucie   Wait.

She goes to the back of her hut. **Jean** *goes back to her table and sits. The hut shrinks to its former size. Then* **Lucie** *returns standing on top of her hut in her wedding dress and veil.* **Jean** *becomes conscious of her behind him and turns to look.*

Jean   In God's name, what do you think you're doing!

Lucie   The last time we were together I undressed. My poor Jean! You're shitting in your pants! I want to move back into the village. You have a house in the village and you haven't much else. I'm prepared to buy now a share of your house until I'm dead, and I will pay you straightaway in cash. The rest of my savings I'm keeping for myself. Does that interest you?

Jean   The house is too small. The way you live is not the way I could live. At my age I'm not going to change.

Lucie   I can change.

Jean Why don't you rent a whole house to yourself? Have you asked anyone else to take you in?

Lucie Only *you* know me!

Jean What you really want, what you have always wanted, is for me to marry you!

Lucie Yes. In church, with this veil.

Jean You are out of your mind.

Lucie *comes down the ladder.*

Lucie There's no one to stop you this time. You are alone.

She touches his hand.

Jean I can't marry you.

Lucie Jean!

Jean Again she said my name as she had said it forty years before and again it separated me, marked me out from all other men. In the pause between her twice saying my name in the same way, I saw myself as the young boy I had once been, encouraged by Masson to believe that I was more than usually intelligent; I saw myself as a young man without prospects, because I was the youngest, but with great ambitions, I saw my first departure for Paris which so impressed me as the centre, the capital of the globe, that I was determined to take one of the roads from L'Étoile across the world, I saw the last goodbyes to my family, my mother imploring me not to go all the time that I harnessed the horse and my father put my bag in the cart. America is the Land of the Dead, she said. I saw myself on the boat on which each day I dreamt of how I would return to the village, honoured and rich with presents for my mother. I saw myself on the quayside where I did not understand a single word of what was being

said, and the great boulevards and the obelisk, the
grandeur of the packing plants which I tried to describe
in a letter to my father, for whom the selling of one cow
for meat was the subject of a month's discussion. I saw
the letter with the news of my father's death, I heard
the noise of the trains through the window of the room
where I lodged for five years, the epidemic in the
shanty town and the carts bearing away the putrid
bodies. Oh, the land of straight railways so flat and
going on for ever; I saw myself in the train going south
to Rio Gallegos in Patagonia, sheep-shearing and a
wind that, like my homesickness, never stopped. I saw
my wedding in Mar del Plata with all seventy-five
members of Ursula's family. I saw the birth of my boys
and my fight with Ursula to christen Basil Basil. I saw
the failure of my marriage, my flight to Montreal, the
boys learning English, a language which I could never
speak, the buying of my bar, the news of Ursula's
death, the news of my mother's death, the fire in the
bar, the police investigations, my Sundays in the forest.
I saw myself working for years as a night-watchman,
the buying of my ticket home . . . I saw forty whole
years compressed within the pause. I looked at her
wrinkled cider-apple face and I hated her. She made
me see my life as wasted. Yet I was forced for the first
and last time in this life to speak to her tenderly. (*To*
Lucie.) Give me time to think, Lucie.

Lucie   Come and tell me when you want to, Jean.

Jean *leaves the hut. The hut dissolves. The table goes down.*

Jean   Before I could give her my considered answer,
she was dead.

Lucie *is lifted above the table, blood streaming from her*
wedding veil. She is dumped in her bathtub coffin which is slid
under her. The funeral procession begins.

Her body was discovered by the postman who noticed that the window onto the road was broken and swinging on its hinges. She had been felled with an axe. The blade had split her skull. The signs were that she had put up a struggle. Her money, her two million was never found.

10   Lucie's funeral

Jean (*continued*) Her death was a kind of disgrace for the village. There were fewer than fifty people at her funeral. There were many flowers on the coffin and the large unsigned wreath I had ordered was not immediately remarkable.

Lucie *sits up in her coffin.*

Lucie Do you want me to say who did it? You can hear me if I say, can't you, Jean?

Jean Yes.

Lucie He's among you, he's here in the cemetery, the thief.

Jean You mean the murderer.

Lucie It's the thief whom I cannot forgive!

Jean It wasn't me.

Lucie You thought of killing me. My brothers look solemn and hopeful, don't they? Solemn and hopeful! Did you decide not to marry me?

Jean I hadn't decided.

Lucie Then I'll wait till you've made up your mind.

The procession stops.

Jean Lucie? Lucie.

They lower the bathtub and cross themselves. **Jean** *peers into the bathtub, trying to find* **Lucie**.

Lucie. Lucie, I . . .

He sits on a chair the chorus provide. The table is placed over the bathtub. A plate in front of him. His room.

She waited. She waited until Hallowe'en!

Lucie I've learnt something, Jean.

He starts and drops his spoon.

All over the world the dead drink on All Saints' Day. Everyone drinks, no one refuses.

Around the edges of the space, the chorus of the dead drink.

Every year it is the same, they drink until they're drunk. They know that they have to visit the living. And so they get drunk! On eau-de-vie!

Jean You sound drunk now.

Lucie (*appearing from her coffin under the table*) Why did you want to kill me?

Jean You are drunk.

Lucie I know why you thought of killing me.

Jean If you know, why do you ask?

Lucie I want to hear you say it.

She gets out of her coffin and stands in front of him. He can't see her and addresses himself to where he last heard her.

Jean Yes, I thought of killing you the night you dressed up. Have you been to see the man who did kill you?

Lucie It doesn't interest me.

Jean You said you could never forgive the thief.

Lucie I've changed my mind. I don't need my savings now. Why did you think of killing me?

Jean Because . . . you were going to force me to marry you.

She drags her bathtub coffin from under the table.

Lucie Force you! Force you! What with? (*Shaking it, she goes off up right.*) What with?

Jean Lucie . . . Lucie . . . Lucie!

11   Blueberry picking

Jean (*continued*) She didn't come back the next day. Nor the next night when I spoke to her. She didn't come back in the autumn, nor the winter, nor the following spring. Nor on St Lucie's day, her name day, the shortest day. At last the weather turned warm. My circulation improved. The old man's blood responding a little to the sun. The apple trees blossomed, the potatoes were planted, the cows were put out to pasture in the alpage, the hay was cut. The next fine day, I told myself, I will climb up to the alpage, past Lucie's chalet, to pick some blueberries.

The dead support sloping planks to make the hillside. The sound of cicadas. **Jean** *picks.*

Jean The mist hung below me making the valley look like the laundry of the damned. Her chalet, long since deserted, looked like a shipwreck.

Lucie Jean! Jean! How many have you picked?

Their voices echo in the mountains.

Jean Half a bucket.

Lucie As slow as ever!

Jean I have calluses under my chin because all my life I have rested it on the handle of a shovel.

Lucie *laughs. The sound becomes the cry of a jackdaw.* **Jean** *looks for her but can't see her.*

Jean Lucie! Lucie!

Lucie Je-an!

He looks up. She is further up the slopes (the back wall), climbing quickly.

Jean Lucie!

Lucie Look, Jean, cherry stones in the birdshit. They fly with them all the way up here! Follow me.

Jean Lucie! Wait for me.

He drops his bucket which clatters all the way down the mountainside, carried by one of the dead. He follows **Lucie** *up the slopes.* **Lucie** *leads him down the other side of the wall. The dead, forming the branches of the forest, help her down. He seems hindered by them, has to brush them aside. They go to the table, centre. She turns, revealed all in white and young again, and drops the other side and lies down.*

Lucie Can you see me now?

Jean Yes.

Lucie How old am I?

Jean You were in the class of 1908. That makes you sixty-eight – no, sixty-seven.

Lucie I was born in the morning. My father was milking in the stable. White cloud like smoke was blowing through the door. My mother had her sister and a neighbour with her. I was born very quickly.

Jean *lies beside her.*

Jean You know everything about your life now.

Lucie If I told you all that I know it would take sixty-seven years.

She gets up.

Come on, Jean.

Lucie *takes* **Jean** *by the hand and leads him downstage. The sound of hammering begins. Behind them the dead are building.*

12   Building the chalet

Jean Where are we?

Lucie This is where I am going to build.

Jean Who does it belong to?

Lucie Me. The dead own everything. I have land now. Land but no seasons.

Worker Lucie!

As they turn to face the builders, **Marius** *comes towards them.*

Marius Fifteen spruces for the columns, a dozen for the purlins, forty twenty-year-old trees for the rafters.

Jean Marius!

Marius I forget how many for the planks. We cut them all down when the axe entered her head. She told us afterwards she heard us sawing in the forest.

Lucie That's when I brought them cheese and cider.

Armand (*dead*) The minute I died I couldn't stop eating!

Marius *introduces the workers.*

Marius You remember Armand. He starved to death in 1924. Georges, who electrocuted himself because he knew he'd become a pauper.

Georges I didn't mean to disturb anyone. I hitched myself up to a high-tension cable. When I died all the lights in the village went out.

Marius Joset who was lost in an avalanche.

Joset That was a great death.

Marius And Mathieu who was struck by lightning.

Mathieu *waves.*

Jean Why are they all here?

Lucie They've come to help us.

Jean Why only –

Lucie Only what, Jean?

Jean The ones who died violently.

Lucie There are not so many who die in their beds. It's a poor country.

Jean Am I to die violently?

She kisses him.

Jean Who are you building the chalet for?

Marius You are warmer in bed with a wife, Jean. The whole war I thought of nothing else, I thought only of caressing La Mélanie in bed. There were some who had intercourse with donkeys, it never interested me, a beast isn't soft enough. When at last I came home I took her to bed and we had our fourth child. Even when I was old and lost my warmth, I thought of going to bed when I was working alone in the fields and sometimes thinking about it made me warm. It was my idea of happiness, you'll see for yourself, if you don't see now – it's better than sleeping alone.

Jean But me and the Cocadrille –

Marius The Cocadrille? It's now she's at the marrying age. Why else would I be building a chalet for her?

Jean You were never a master builder and sixty-seven is no marrying age!

Marius We can become anything. That's why injustice is impossible here. There may be the accident of birth but there is no accident of death. Nothing forces us to stay what we were. The Cocadrille could be seventeen, tall, with wide hips and with breasts you couldn't take your eyes off – only then you wouldn't know her as the Cocadrille, would you? You see all these men here. They have married her!

Jean Not Georges!

Marius Georges was the first. He married her the day after her funeral. The bridesmaids took the flowers from the grave. Those who die violently fall into each other's arms.

Jean So I am to die violently.

Marius Do you want to marry her? Do you want to marry her?

Worker Everything's ready!

Jean's *moment of decision. He takes off his jacket and goes to help the workers build. They cheer. They get ready to raise the central support of the chalet, which lies on the floor.* **Mathieu** *assigns everyone a position. All kneel and wrap their arms around the beam.*

Marius You cradle the wood like you'd cradle a baby. (*He encourages them.*) Tchee tchee hissss. Tchee tchee hissss. Tchee tchee hissss.

They lift.

Marius Put your forearm under it. Tchee tchee hissss. Tchee tchee hissss.

The beam is lifted.

Marius Get your shoulder under it. Tchee tchee hissss. Tchee tchee hissss.

They support the beam on their shoulders. Pause.

Jean Yes, I should have married her.

They continue lifting.

Marius Tchee tchee hissss. Quick, get the pole. Put the pole under it. Tchee tchee hissss.

Mathieu *puts a support pole behind the beam which is almost upright now. The workers groan with the effort and hold the beam for one last time as it goes into position. It drops into its hole on their last shout.* **Lucie** *appears.*

Jean I will marry you.

Cheers. Chairs are brought. **Lucie** *and* **Jean** *sit.*

Armand You took your time!

Lucie You should talk. You've lived alone all your life, you get drunk alone and you smell like a distillery. Jean has been to the other side of the world, he married, he had children, he came back, he picks blueberries very slowly, all right he pretends to be deaf and he wanted to kill me, but now at the last moment, the very last moment, he has agreed to marry me. You would never have the spunk to do that!

The workers go back to work raising the two smaller beams.

Jean I thought the dead rested after a lifetime's work.

Lucie When they remember their past they work. What else should they do?

Jean I must help them.

Lucie They don't need any help.

Jean But we need some food for them, and drink to celebrate, we need –

Lucie Everything's prepared.

Jean But I don't see any tables or –

Lucie Look – they've almost finished. So, my contraband – I've smuggled you here.

Marius *comes to them with the bouquet.*

Marius Do you want to nail the bouquet?

Jean Yes, I will nail the bouquet.

Jean *climbs the ladder placed against the beam.* **Lucie** *follows him. She sings. The dead join in.*

Lucie
   Apricagot de lee nay-a
   Sopiyay-a, *etc.*

Jean *reaches the top of the beam. There is a man the other side.*

Jean Who are you?

Man Lucie knew me as St Just.

Jean You were in the Maquis!

St Just We were ordered to dig our graves and then we were shot.

Jean I will tell you something. After the Liberation, there were Nazis who escaped and came to the Argentine, and there they lived off the fat of the pampas.

St Just They only escaped for a moment.

Jean How can you be so sure?

St Just Justice will be done.

Jean When?

St Just When the living know what the dead suffered.

Jean *nails the bouquet to the top of the beam.* **Lucie** *turns.*

Lucie Wait for me.

She goes down slowly and goes off. All watch. The dead sing. But their singing is distorted and weak. They seem to be fading. Light fades. **Jean** *tries to make out where* **Lucie** *is. He is frightened. Suddenly, the ladder disappears from under him. The tile shingles on the back wall begin to fall.*

Jean Lucie! Lucie!

More shingles fall. **Jean** *clings to the beam as he falls. Everything collapses around him. Darkness. As he hits the floor and rolls, the back wall, a skeleton of wooden struts now, falls forward slowly and comes to rest on the two smaller beams left and right.*

Epilogue

Jean *goes to the stove right and sits.*

Jean Before I was six, perhaps I was only two or three, I used to watch my father in the kitchen on winter mornings, when it was still as dark as night. He knelt by an iron beast, feeding it. Now when I light the stove in the morning, I say to myself: I and the fire are the only living things in this house; my father, mother, brothers, sisters, the horses, cows, rabbits, chickens, all have gone. And Lucie Cabrol is dead. I say this, and I do not altogether believe it. Sometimes it seems to me that I am nearing the edge of the forest. I will never again be sixteen. If I am to leave the forest, it will be on the far side. But there are moments when I see something different.

The dead appear and lower the central beam so it rests like the others against the fallen back wall, making the slope of a roof.

Moments when a blue sky reminds me of Lucie Cabrol.

Blue backlight throws the roof into relief.

Then I see again the roof which we raised, built from the trees. And then I am convinced that when I leave the forest I will leave it with the love of the Cocadrille.

Music. Fade.